AN IMAGINATION LIBRARY SERIES

WORLD'S LARGEST
SNAKES

Boa Constrictors

by Valerie J. Weber

Gareth Stevens Publishing
A WORLD ALMANAC EDUCATION GROUP COMPANY

Please visit our web site at: www.garethstevens.com
For a free color catalog describing Gareth Stevens Publishing's
list of high-quality books and multimedia programs,
call 1-800-542-2595 (USA) or 1-800-387-3178 (Canada).
Gareth Stevens Publishing's fax: (414) 332-3567.

Library of Congress Cataloging-in-Publication Data available upon request
from publisher. Fax (414) 336-0157 for the attention of the Publishing
Records Department.

ISBN 0-8368-3654-5

First published in 2003 by
Gareth Stevens Publishing
A World Almanac Education Group Company
330 West Olive Street, Suite 100
Milwaukee, WI 53212 USA

Text: Valerie J. Weber
Cover design and page layout: Scott M. Krall
Series editor: Jim Mezzanotte
Picture Researcher: Diane Laska-Swanke

Photo credits: Cover © François Gohier/Ardea London Ltd.; pp. 5, 7, 11 © Joe McDonald/Visuals
Unlimited; p. 9 © Jim Merli/Visuals Unlimited; pp. 13, 15 © Chris Mattison; pp. 17, 21
© Brian Kenney; p. 19 © John Cancalosi/naturepl.com

Printed in the United States of America

1 2 3 4 5 6 7 8 9 07 06 05 04 03

Front cover: **A boa constrictor has a flexible backbone with more than a hundred bones. Your backbone has thirty-three bones.**

TABLE OF CONTENTS

Words that appear in the glossary are printed in **boldface** type the first time they occur in the text.

A Tiny Giant

While most of the world's giant snakes can be more than 20 feet (6 meters) long, boa constrictors rarely stretch out to more than 13 feet (4 m). The boa's vast **range** is probably more impressive than its length. This range extends from northwestern Mexico to Argentina in South America, and it also includes islands located off the coast of Central and South America.

Like many other giant snakes, boa constrictors live in **tropical** rain forests, but they also **slither** through grasslands, farmers' fields, and even along desert rocks and sands.

This boa constrictor winds its way around a tree branch in a South American forest. Like all giant snakes, boa constrictors are very strong.

The Colorful Constrictor

Boa constrictors come in many colors and sizes. Scientists are not sure if there is only one kind of boa constrictor, with many **variations**, or a lot of different kinds of boas. Boas can have coloring that varies from tan to brown. They may have patches on their backs in different shades of brown and white, or they may be mostly gray or silver with brown or red patches. A boa's color is lightest at its head and gets gradually darker toward its tail.

If you stroked a boa constrictor from head to tail, its **scales** would feel smooth and dry. If you stroked a boa in the opposite direction, its scales would feel rough. Either way, you would feel the boa's powerful muscles beneath its skin!

The coloring on this South American boa constrictor is light around the head but gets quite dark near the snake's tail.

Jacobson's Organ

Like all snakes, the boa constrictor uses its tongue to gather information about the smells surrounding it. As a boa constrictor flicks its tongue from side to side, it gathers tiny **scent** particles on its tongue. The snake then transfers these particles to the Jacobson's **organ** on the roof of its mouth.

The Jacobson's organ sends information to the boa constrictor's brain. Using this information, the boa's brain can tell what is close by — dinner, danger, or maybe even a mate.

This red-tailed boa constrictor must be sensing danger from either humans or animals. Many snakes open their mouths wide when they are alarmed.

What's for Dinner?

Boas are comfortable on the ground or in trees, and they hunt a variety of **prey**. They mostly feed on **warm-blooded** animals, from rodents such as rats to birds they find on the ground and on the lower branches of trees.

As a boa constrictor grows larger, it has more trouble climbing trees, so it often waits on the ground for an animal to pass. Besides rodents and birds, boas also eat lizards, squirrels, rabbits, and small wild pigs. Boas often live close to farms and houses, which give them a convenient source for chickens, ducks, or a family's cat or small dog!

By pushing its belly scales against branches, this South American boa constrictor can climb trees in its forest home.

A Quick Death

A rat passes by a boa constrictor. With a quick snap, the boa has the animal in its mouth. The snake wraps the upper part of its body around the rat. The boa's movement is so fast you can hardly see it. The rat barely struggles — only one small squeak escapes its mouth. Then it is motionless.

A boa constrictor does not kill its victims by crushing their bones. Instead, a boa constricts, or squeezes, its prey until the animal **suffocates**, unable to draw a breath as the snake tightens its **coils**. The rat's lungs cannot expand against the strength of the boa's muscles, so it cannot breathe.

Since a snake swallows its dinner whole and does not chew, not much blood shows as it pulls its prey into its mouth.

"Rubber Band" Jaws

A boa constrictor usually tries to eat prey such as a rat by swallowing the head first. If the snake started at the rat's tail, the rat's limbs would stick out on either side of the boa's mouth, making it hard for the snake to swallow.

Unlike human jaws, which are joined at the back, a boa's jaws are connected only by a **tendon**, which acts like a rubber band. The tendon stretches as the snake widens its mouth over its prey. A boa constrictor can eat a meal much larger than its own head — in one gulp!

After getting its prey completely into its mouth, this boa constrictor will kink its neck to help push down its dinner. A lot of spit helps ease the way!

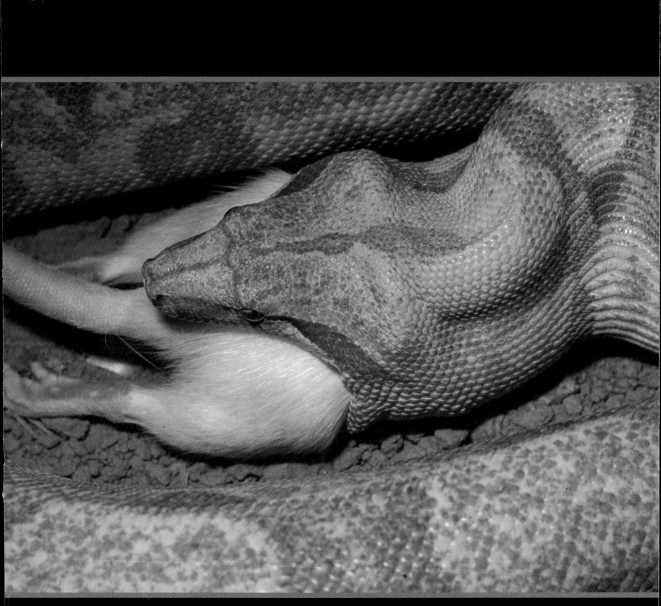

Baby Boas

Unlike many other snakes, boa constrictors give birth to live young rather than lay eggs. A female boa will give birth to eleven to sixty young snakes at a time, usually in the late summer or early autumn. A newborn boa is a fully formed snake. It can be 18 to 24 inches (46 to 61 cm) long and may double in length in a year.

Once the baby snakes are born, their mother pays no attention to them — they are on their own and ready to hunt. Baby boas are ready to have babies themselves in two to three years.

A newborn boa constrictor tries to break open the sac in which it was born. Most baby boas are able to break free of their sacs within an hour of birth.

A Movie Star

You know those big snakes slithering from the trees in jungle movies? Whatever kind of snake they are supposed to be in the movies, they are usually boa constrictors in real life. Boas are often used in films because they are gentle and easy to handle. Special camera angles and backdrops are used to make the snakes appear larger than they really are.

With careful handling, a boa constrictor also can make a good pet. Of course, you would never want to get in its way when it was hungry!

With the right care and feeding, a boa constrictor can make a great pet. Boa constrictors can live for twenty years or more.

Threats to the Boa

For many animals, boa constrictors are dangerous neighbors. But these snakes face their own dangers. Animals such as birds and lizards, for example, will eat baby boa constrictors. The boa's worst enemies, however, are people. Like all the giant snakes, boas are a **threatened species**.

People kill the boa constrictor for its skin or meat or simply because they are afraid of snakes. When people build roads, farms, and towns, the **habitats** of boa constrictors are often reduced. As the hunting grounds of these snakes shrink, they may find it hard to find food.

This red-eyed tree frog does not look like it is worried, but it should be. The boa constrictor could kill this small animal as quick as lightning!

MORE TO READ AND VIEW

Books (Nonfiction)   *Boa Constrictors. Animals of the Rain Forest* (series). Sam Dollar
(Raintree/Steck-Vaughn)
Boa Constrictors. Rain Forest Animals (series). Helen Frost
(Pebble Books)
Boa Constrictors. Snakes (series). James E. Gerholdt
(Checkerboard Library)
Boa Constrictors and Other Boas. Snakes (series). James Martin
and Mary Ann McDonald (Capstone Press)
Boas: The Really Wild Life of Boas. Really Wild Life of Snakes (series).
Doug Wechsler (Powerkids Press)
Fangs! (series). Eric Ethan (Gareth Stevens)

Books (Fiction)   *To Bathe a Boa.* C. Imbior Kudrna (Lerner Publishing)
The Day Jimmy's Boa Ate the Wash. Trinka Hakes Noble (Bt Bound)

Videos (Nonfiction)   *Animal Life for Children: All About Reptiles.* (Schlessinger Media)
Fascinating World of Snakes. (Tapeworm)
Predators of the Wild: Snake. (Warner Studios)
Snakes: The Ultimate Guide. (Discovery Home Video)

PLACES TO WRITE AND VISIT

Here are three places to contact for more information:

Black Hills Reptile Gardens
P.O. Box 620
Rapid City, SD 57709
USA
1-800-355-0275
www.reptile-gardens.com

Oakland Zoo
9777 Golf Links Road
Oakland, CA 94605
USA
1-510-632-9525
www.oaklandzoo.org

Sedgwick County Zoo
5555 Zoo Boulevard
Wichita, KS 67212
USA
1-316-942-2217
www.scz.org

WEB SITES

Web sites change frequently, but we believe the following web sites are going to last. You can also use good search engines, such as **Yahooligans!** [**www.yahooligans.com**] or **Google** [**www.google.com**], to find more information about boa constrictors. Here are some keywords to help you: *boa constrictors*, *boas*, *Jacobson's organ*, *rain forest animals*, *reptiles*, and *snakes*.

www.bio.davidson.edu/Biology/herpcons/ Myths/Modern_Myths.html
Do snakes hypnotize their victims? Do they travel in pairs? At this site, you will learn what is fact and what is fiction!

www.enchantedlearning.com/subjects/ reptiles/snakes/Boa.shtm/
Visit this site to see how a boa constrictor eats its prey. The drawing at this web site needs your artistic touch. Print it out and put your crayons to work.

http://jajhs.kana.k12.wv.us/amazon/ boas.htm
At this site, you will learn about the size and habits of boa constrictors.

www.oaklandzoo.org/atoz/azboa.html
This page from the web site of the Oakland Zoo has a picture of a boa constrictor and provides many facts about this giant snake.

GLOSSARY

You can find these words on the pages listed. Reading a word in a sentence helps you understand it even better.

coils (KOYLZ) — the circles a snake can form with its body 12

habitats (HAB-uh-tatz) — places where an animal or plant lives 20

organ (OR-gun) — a part of the body that does a particular job 8

prey (PRAY) — animals that are hunted by other animals for food 10, 12, 14

range (RAYNJ) — the entire area where a particular animal might be found 4

scales (SKAYLZ) — small, stiff plates, made mostly of the same material as human hair and nails, that cover a snake's skin 6, 10

scent (SENT) — a particular smell, such as the smell of a certain animal 8

slither (SLITH-ur) — move by sliding 4, 18

suffocates (SUF-uh-kaytz) — dies from having no air to breathe 12

tendon (TEN-dun) — a strong, flexible band of tissue that attaches a muscle to a bone 14

threatened species (THRET-end SPEESH-eez) — plants or animals of a certain kind that are in danger of dying out 20

tropical (TROP-ih-cull) — being in a part of the world where the temperature is always warm and plants usually grow year-round 4

variations (vair-ee-AY-shunz) — different forms of something 6

warm-blooded (WARM blud-id) — having blood that stays at the same temperature, even when the air temperature outside the body changes 10

INDEX